Make Your Own Art

Papier-Mâché

Sally Henry and Trevor Cook

PowerKiDS press.

New York

Published in 2011 by The Rosen Publishing Group, Inc.
29 East 21st Street, New York, NY 10010

Text and design: Sally Henry and Trevor Cook
Editor: Joe Harris
U.S. editor: Kara Murray
Photography: Sally Henry and Trevor Cook

Library of Congress Cataloging-in-Publication Data

Henry, Sally.
 Papier-mâché / by Sally Henry and Trevor Cook.
    p. cm. — (Make your own art)
 Includes index.
 ISBN 978-1-4488-1587-6 (library binding) — ISBN 978-1-4488-1621-7 (pbk.) —
 ISBN 978-1-4488-1622-4 (6-pack)
 1. Papier-mâché—Juvenile literature. I. Cook, Trevor, 1948– II. Title.
 TT871.H45 2011
 745.54'2—dc22
                        2010024762
Printed in the United States

SL001625US

CPSIA Compliance Information: Batch #WA11PK: For Further Information contact Rosen Publishing, New York, New York at 1-800-237-9932

Contents

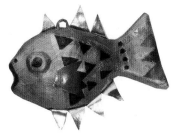

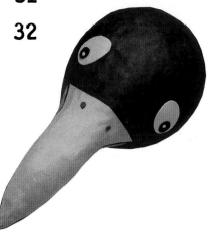

Introduction

Papier-mâché (sounds like **pay-per muh-SHAY**) is a name for paper and glue layered together to make a strong, stiff material. It's very light and strong, and, even better, it doesn't cost a lot of money!

Paper

The best kind of paper to use for most of our projects is ordinary **newspaper**. Tear it into strips about 2 by 1 inch (50 x 25 mm), smaller for fine detail, bigger for large flat areas. Tear rather than cut your paper: it will be smoother.

Brush glue evenly but sparingly onto the paper. Lay down each strip so that it slightly overlaps its neighbor.

Make sure that there are no air bubbles trapped between the layers. Five layers should be strong enough for most purposes. Allow plenty of time for the glue to dry.

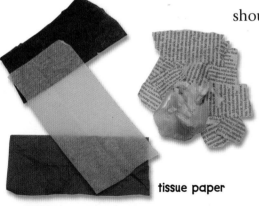

tissue paper

You can quickly bulk up the details in your pâpier-mâché project by crumpling up **tissue paper**. Mix in a little white glue, scrunch it up, then cover it over with newspaper.

Glue

We've used a glue called **white glue** to make our papier-mâché. It's white, but turns clear when it's dry. We've also used this to glue objects together. It makes paper stiff but flexible. If you want your jar of white glue to last longer, you can mix two parts white glue with one part water.

white glue

Card stock and cardboard

Shapes cut from **card stock** or **cardboard** often form the starting point for a project in papier-mâché. Card stock is bendable, like thick paper. Cardboard is thicker, stronger and more rigid, and is often made of layers of card stock.

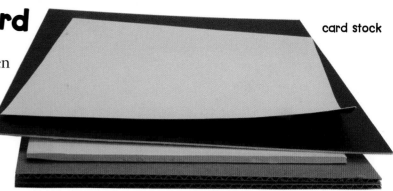

card stock

cardboard

Paint and varnish

Any water-based **paint** is fine to use. Bright colors often work best when painted on a white background. It's a good idea to paint over papier-mâché made of newspaper with water-based white household paint and allow it to dry before painting in colors.

When the colors have dried, make them brighter by giving your work a coat of **varnish**. Pictures, like the one on pages 22–23, look better with a matte varnish. Things that need to be hard, such as the desk organizer on pages 20–21, should be finished with a glossy varnish. Special paper varnish is ideal, but you can use ordinary water-based household varnishes instead. When painting or varnishing an object all over, it's important to prevent it from coming into contact with other surfaces as it dries. To stop things from sticking to each other, cover them in stages, hanging them up to dry if possible.

water-based paints

Soft materials

felt

Felt and **fun foam** (sometimes called craft foam) can be found in craft shops. Both come in bright colors and are alternatives to painting. Cut out details, such as the eyes on the monster bird on pages 14–15, and stick them on with glue.

fun foam

Elastic

Sometimes you need to hang things up so they'll bounce a little! Use **elastic cord** for the octopus on pages 26–27 and the piñata on pages 28–29.

To hold the monster heads on pages 14–15 on properly, you might need some **elastic braid**.

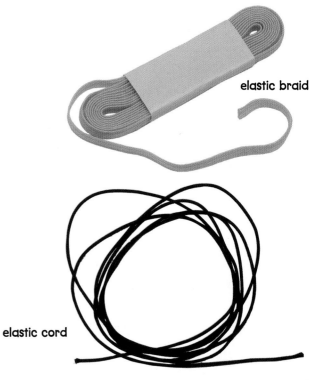

elastic braid

elastic cord

string

nylon line

Tying things up

Along with ordinary packing **string**, we use **nylon line** for some of our projects. It's sometimes used for fishing, but you can get it in short lengths from craft shops. Use a lightweight piece for the fish mobile on pages 18–19.

Wire

To make hanging loops for the fish, piñata, and octopus, we've used wire **paper clips**. The piggy's tail on page 8 is built around a large paper clip that's been twisted with pliers. Get an adult to help you with this.

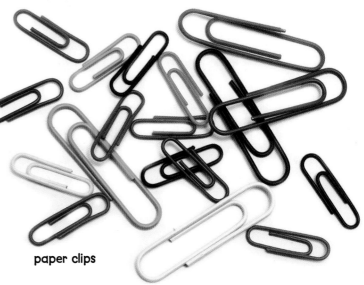

paper clips

Tools

Even though we've made all the newspaper strips by tearing, we still need **scissors** for all the projects in this book. Choose a pair with rounded ends. They're safer!

safety scissors

You will need to have an adult around to help you with some of these tools. Get a grown-up to show you the best way to use a **craft knife** to cut the corks on page 9, for example.

pliers

craft knife

Bending wire paper clips is easy with **pliers** like these.

paper punch

A **paper punch** makes neat holes in paper. The little round shapes it cuts can look great when they're stuck together in a pattern!

Sometimes it's good to fix card stock and cardboard together with **staples** before covering them with paper.

Clean and safe

stapler

Find **somewhere to work** that's easy to clean. Glue is hard to get off, so avoid carpets, curtains, and furry pets. A kitchen is an ideal place, but be sure to ask first. Sometimes there's other work to be done there! Before you start, cover your working area with clean newspapers. Ensure you have enough space for things to stand while glue, paint, or varnish dries.

Piggy Bank

Our papier-mâché piggy bank's a lot
tougher than an old-fashioned china one!

3 HOURS

10 MINUTES

You will need:

- *One round balloon • Old newspapers*
- *White glue • Air-drying modeling clay*
- *Two corks • Paper clip*
- *Small plastic bottle • Wobbly eyes*
- *Paints • Scissors • Thumbtack*
- *Craft knife • Pliers • Paintbrushes*

What to do...

We're going to build the piggy bank around a
balloon. Think about how much you want to
save, then make sure your balloon is big enough.
Be patient. You shouldn't break your piggy bank
open until it's full!

8

1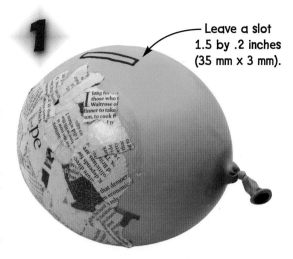

Leave a slot 1.5 by .2 inches (35 mm x 3 mm).

Blow up the balloon to about 6 inches (150 mm) across. Cover it with five layers of paper and white glue but leave a narrow slot uncovered.

2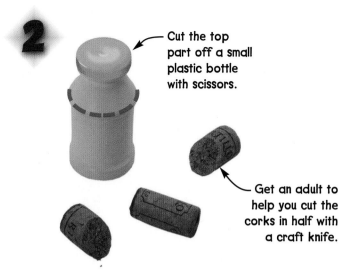

Cut the top part off a small plastic bottle with scissors.

Get an adult to help you cut the corks in half with a craft knife.

Cut two corks in half for legs, and cut the top off a plastic bottle to make a snout.

3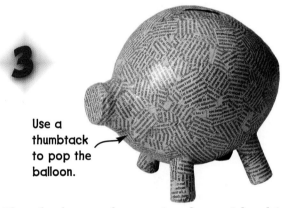

Use a thumbtack to pop the balloon.

Glue the legs and snout in place with white glue. When it has dried, add more papier-mâché.

4

Make some ears from air-drying modeling clay and cover them with paper and glue.

5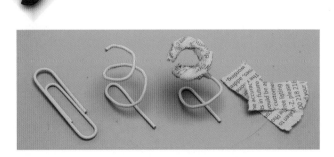

Ask an adult to help you twist a paper clip into a curly tail, using a pair of pliers. Wrap it with paper and glue. Attach it to the end opposite the snout with more papier-mâché.

6

Now paint your piggy bank. When it's dry, glue on wobbly eyes, and paint or glue on nostrils and a mouth. Happy saving!

Maracas

These musical instruments are very easy to make and even easier to play!

2 HOURS

10 MINUTES

You will need:

- *Two round balloons*
- *Two small plastic bottles*
- *White glue* • *Old newspapers*
- *Paints* • *Paintbrushes*
- *Colored markers*
- *Dried beans (or peas)*
- *Paper varnish*
- *Scissors* • *Thumbtacks*

What to do...

Maracas are percussion instruments from Latin America. They are made from hollow shells, filled with something that will make a noise when shaken.

We're going to make our maracas out of paper, with dried beans inside. There are instructions here for making one, but it's best to have a pair, and shake one in each hand. Practice shaking them in time with some music!

1

Blow up a balloon to about 6 inches (150 mm) in diameter. Glue on five layers of paper, but leave the neck uncovered.

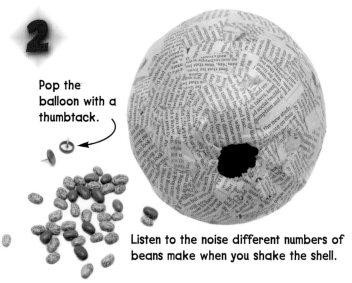

2

Pop the balloon with a thumbtack.

Listen to the noise different numbers of beans make when you shake the shell.

When the paper is dry, pop the balloon and remove it. Put some dried beans (or peas) into the shell through the hole.

3

Glue extra paper here.

You can use a bottle like this one.

Fix a small plastic bottle in place over the hole with white glue. Cover the bottle in five layers of papier-mâché, and strengthen it with about ten layers. Allow all the glue to dry completely.

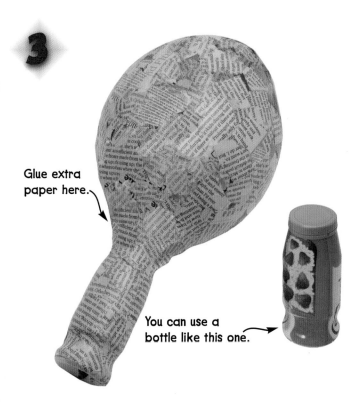

4

Draw a pattern with a marker. Fill in the pattern with paint in bright colors. When the paint has dried, finish it off with a coat of varnish. Now you're ready for a fiesta!

Turtle Bowl

A fun and useful gift that looks great and costs very little to make.

2 HOURS

10 MINUTES

You will need:

- *One round balloon*
- *White glue*
- *Old newspapers • Stiff card stock*
- *Paints • Brushes*
- *Varnish*
- *Wobbly eyes*
- *Markers*
- *Tissue paper*
- *Scissors*

What to do...

We're going to make a turtle with an upside-down shell. It can be used as a decorative bowl and would make a great present for someone!

You could use it to store all sorts of things. It would be a great place to keep wrapped candies, keys, or marbles.

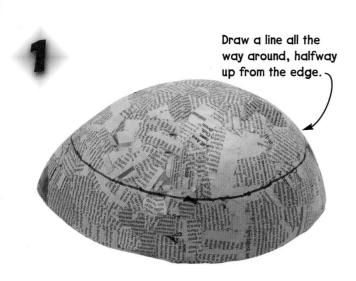

1

Draw a line all the way around, halfway up from the edge.

Cover half a balloon with five layers of paper. Allow it to dry, then pop the balloon. Neaten the edge with scissors, and strengthen it with extra paper. When it's dry, draw a line about halfway up.

2

Carefully cut along the line with scissors to divide the shell into two parts. Turn the top part over and fit it into the lower part. Stick the two halves together with paper and glue.

3

fold

glue

glue

glue

glue

glue

glue

Copy these head, legs, and tail shapes onto stiff card stock and cut them out. Fold at the dotted line. Use crumpled tissue paper mixed with glue to pad out the upper sides. Cover with glue and paper.

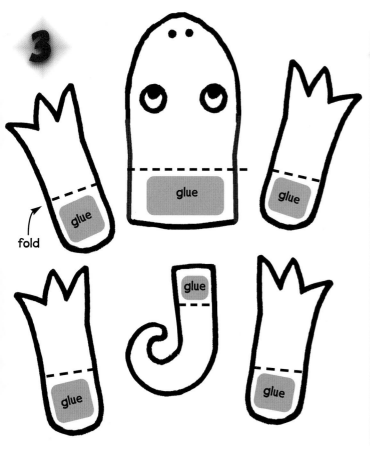

4

You can paint the shell with a pattern you like. It will still look like a turtle!

Fix the head, legs, and tail in place under the shell with white glue. Paint your turtle and finish it off with a coat of varnish. When the varnish is dry, glue on the wobbly eyes.

Monster Heads

You can wear these monster heads as part of a costume. Just add a colorful cloak.

2 HOURS

10 MINUTES

You will need:

- *Two large balloons* • *Old newspapers*
- *Cardboard* • *White glue* • *Plastic bottles*
- *Bubble wrap (for the bird head)*
- *Elastic braid* • *Thumbtack*
- *Paints* • *Brushes* • *Scissors* • *Varnish*
- *Beads* • *Tissue paper* • *Markers*

What to do...

Parties, plays, or parades are perfect occasions for these big masks. Start with a balloon again, but this time you'll need to make sure it is the right size. You're going to need it to be a bit bigger than the head of the person who's going to wear it! Build your favorite monster character for a carnival or trick-or-treat outing on Halloween.

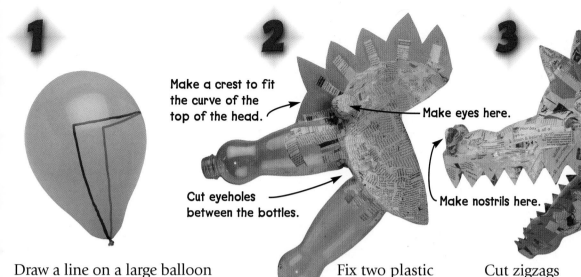

1

Draw a line on a large balloon as shown above. Glue five layers of paper up to the line. Allow it to dry, then pop the balloon with a pin.

2

Make a crest to fit the curve of the top of the head.

Make eyes here.

Cut eyeholes between the bottles.

Fix two plastic bottles to the front with white glue. Add a cardboard crest, eyeholes, and eyes made of balled-up tissue paper. Cover with papier-mâché.

3

Make nostrils here.

Make teeth 1 inch (25 mm) high.

Cut zigzags into two strips of cardboard about 2 inches (50 mm) wide. Glue them onto the bottles, and cover them with papier-mâché.

4

Glass beads make great eyes!

We've painted our dragon red and green, but you could choose any color you like. Fix elastic braid to the edges of the head with staples and finish it off with varnish. Scary!

Here's a monster bird head made in the same way as the dragon, but it's a lot simpler. Its beak is made using only one bottle!

Add layers of bubble wrap to shape the bottle, then cover with paper.

Stick the bottle where the neck end of the balloon was and cover it with extra paper.

This time, the opening for the head is underneath.

Bowling-Pin Soldiers

Ten brave soldiers are standing to attention. Who'll be the first to knock them all down?

2 HOURS

5 MINUTES

You will need:

- Ten drink bottles • Sand
- Old newspaper • White glue
- Colored fabric • Sequins
- Paints • Paintbrushes • Paper
- Beads • Gilt trim • Newspapers
- Tissue paper • Scissors

What to do...

Plastic drink bottles are an ideal size and shape for building bowling pins. Cover them with papier-mâché to make them strong enough to last the game!

1

Fill your bottle with clean, dry sand. Don't forget to put the lid back on the bottle!

2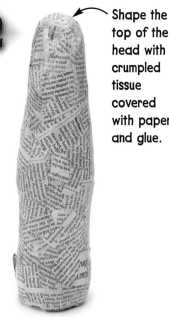

Shape the top of the head with crumpled tissue covered with paper and glue.

Cover the bottle with five layers of paper.

3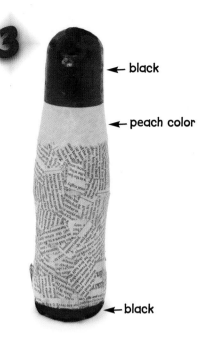

← black

← peach color

← black

Paint the hat, face, and feet.

4

Paint the cheeks. Stick on beads for eyes, a paper triangle for the mouth, and a black paper mustache.

5

Make arms from the same red material, or use card stock if you want to paint your soldiers. →

Paint a dark strip to show that our soldier has two legs!

Wrap the top half of the bowling pin with red material and the bottom half with blue, using white glue to fix it in place. Glue on two fabric arms.

6

Stick on sequins for buttons, a yellow stripe of fabric down the side of the pants, and some gilt trim around the collar. He's done, only nine more to go!

Fantastic Fish

This fun mobile gives a new meaning to the phrase "flying fish!"

2 HOURS

10 MINUTES

You will need:

- *Stiff cardboard* • *Old newspapers* • *White glue*
- *Metallic paints* • *Paintbrushes* • *Scissors*
- *Paper clips* • *Nylon line* • *Wooden skewers*
- *Colored tissue paper* • *Metal foil* • *Beads*

What to do...

You can use papier-mâché to create a sparkly mobile featuring all sorts of exotic sea life. Balance your mobile carefully, and the tiniest movement of air will make the fish dart around.

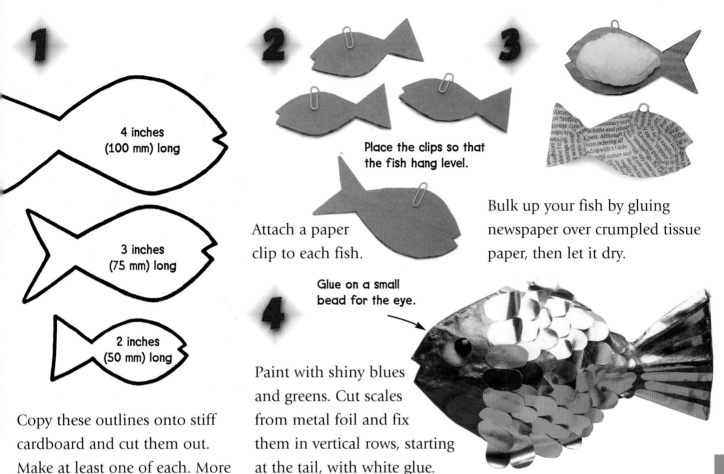

1

4 inches
(100 mm) long

3 inches
(75 mm) long

2 inches
(50 mm) long

Copy these outlines onto stiff cardboard and cut them out. Make at least one of each. More is better!

2

Place the clips so that the fish hang level.

Attach a paper clip to each fish.

3

Bulk up your fish by gluing newspaper over crumpled tissue paper, then let it dry.

4

Glue on a small bead for the eye.

Paint with shiny blues and greens. Cut scales from metal foil and fix them in vertical rows, starting at the tail, with white glue.

19

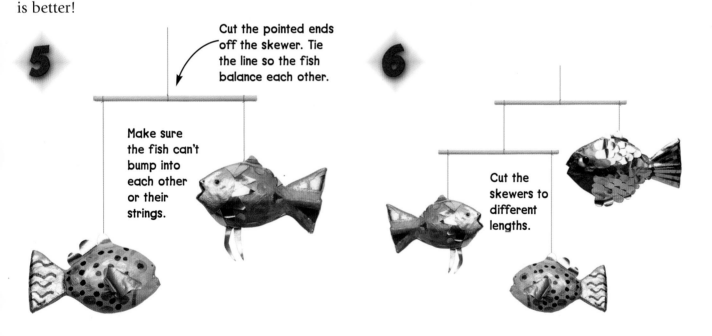

5

Cut the pointed ends off the skewer. Tie the line so the fish balance each other.

Make sure the fish can't bump into each other or their strings.

6

Cut the skewers to different lengths.

Tie a nylon line to the paper clip loop on each fish. Hang a fish from either end of a wooden skewer. Tie another piece of line to the middle of the stick so it balances when it's held up.

Make more pairs of fish. You can attach pairs to sticks and balance pairs with single fish. The more the merrier! Now find somewhere to hang your mobile!

Treasure Island

Let's make an island for all those treasures that don't have a home! It's a handy place for markers, pencils, scissors, and brushes.

60 MINUTES   **5 MINUTES**

You will need:

- *Stiff cardboard* • *Newspapers*
- *Cardboard tubes*
- *Colored tissue paper*
- *White glue* • *Stapler* • *Scissors*
- *Varnish* • *Brush* • *Sequin*

What to do...

How many tubes do you need in your desert island desk organizer? You can include as many as you have objects to organize.

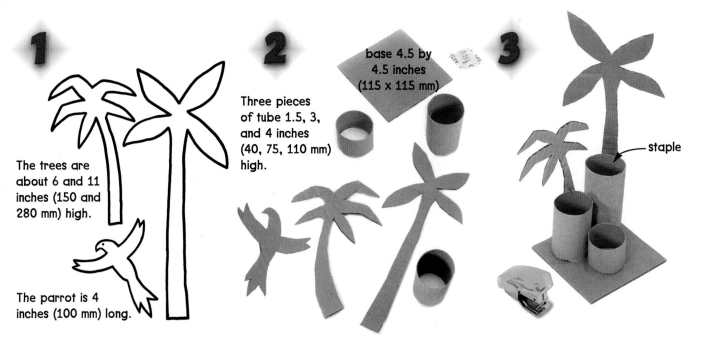

1

The trees are about 6 and 11 inches (150 and 280 mm) high.

The parrot is 4 inches (100 mm) long.

2

base 4.5 by 4.5 inches (115 x 115 mm)

Three pieces of tube 1.5, 3, and 4 inches (40, 75, 110 mm) high.

3

staple

Copy the outline of these trees and the parrot onto cardboard and cut them out.

Use scissors to cut three lengths of tube and a square of cardboard for the base.

Use staples to secure the trees to the back of the tubes. Then glue them onto the base.

4

Paper over balls of tissue for coconuts.

5

Growing coconuts are green!

Glue the parrot to this tree by one wing.

Apply varnish with a soft, clean brush.

Wrap everything with five layers of glued paper. Don't forget the parrot!

Glue on several layers of brightly colored tissue paper, and when it's dry, apply varnish. Glue a sequin on the parrot for an eye, then glue the parrot to the tree by one wing, as in the picture. What a great gift for someone!

Painting with Paper

You can create fabulous colors by building up layers of
colored tissue paper. Let's use it to make a picture!

60
MINUTES

5
MINUTES

You will need:

- *Piece of stiff white cardboard, the backing for your picture*
- *Pencil or waterproof marker (that won't come off on the tissue paper)*
- *Colored tissue paper*
- *White glue • Brushes • Scissors*

What to do...

Start with an idea in your imagination, a view from your window, or a photograph. Make a drawing first, then choose your colors carefully. With care you can make a real work of art!

1 This is white cardboard cut from an old box.

2 Draw with a solid, black line.

Instead of paint, we are using colored tissue paper and glue. For areas of color like the sky, glue flat tissue paper layer on layer, making the color stronger with every piece. To keep the color clear, it's important that you work on a white background.

When you choose your view, look for an interesting feature like the house in our picture. See how the other shapes can draw the eye to it. You can start your work with a drawing of your own, or you can copy ours!

3

These bits of tissue paper are scrunched up and pushed together to look like grass in a field.

These flowers are made by building up the yellow petals around an orange center.

Cut straight-edged shapes like this house from card stock. Color it by sticking on tissue paper with glue.

Use the tissue paper to make different textures in different areas. Be careful. Try to work methodically and keep your picture neat!

4 Let the light background show through as clouds.

If you find the drawing is too detailed, simplify!

Avoid putting dark colors under light ones.

As you cover areas with tissue paper, you may think at first that the color is quite drab. Only when the tissue paper dries out, though, is the full color shown. To get the best results with this method, it's good to work slowly!

Paper Jewelry

Make stunning jewelry out of magazine pictures and glue!

45 MINUTES

5 MINUTES

You will need:

- *Pictures cut from glossy magazines, brochures, or advertising flyers*
- *White glue*
- *Nylon line or elastic cord*
- *Knitting needle – 0.2 inches (3 mm) or size 11 • Glitter • Paint • Paintbrush*
- *Scissors • Newspaper • Beads*
- *Earring clips (optional, from craft store)*

What to do...

The big beads in the picture above are made of tightly rolled paper, stuck with glue. Find pictures in old glossy magazines that have areas of color and patterns that you like. The beads in our necklace have different colors and textures. You can also try working with similar colors or patterns.

1

Find pieces of color and pattern in your pictures and cut them out as strips about .75 to 1.5 inches (20–40 mm) wide.

2

Cut out strips of newspaper the same width to make the body of the bead.

3

Make sure the edges are straight and not torn.

Roll newspaper strips around the knitting needle. Add glue as you go, but be careful not to glue the paper to the needle!

4

You can make lots of beads at once on the same knitting needle.

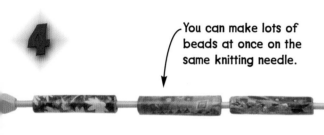

Add strips until the roll is about .5 inch (12 mm) across. Finish with the colorful patterned paper.

5

When the glue is dry, slide the rolls off the needle. Paint the ends of the rolls a matching color.

6

If you use nylon line, make sure the necklace is big enough to go over your head!

Add a little glitter! →

Thread the rolls onto nylon line or elastic cord. We've added a small bead between each one. Finish by tying the ends together.

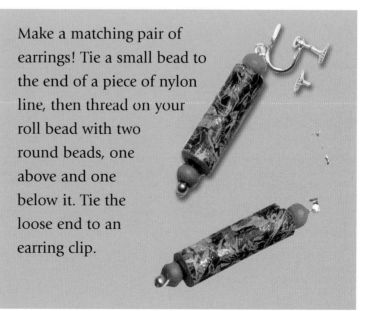

Make a matching pair of earrings! Tie a small bead to the end of a piece of nylon line, then thread on your roll bead with two round beads, one above and one below it. Tie the loose end to an earring clip.

Octopus

This fun and unusual hanging room decoration will surprise your friends!

3 HOURS

10 MINUTES

You will need:

- Round balloon • Four modeling balloons • Old newspapers
- Thin card stock • White glue
- Corks • Colored tissue paper • Thumbtack
- String • Elastic cord • Stapler
- Paints • Brushes • Craft knife (to slice through cork)
- Paper clip • Wobbly eyes
- Scissors • Paper punch

What to do...

With eight legs and a huge head, there's a lot of work to do to make this creature and some patience is needed. We think you'll enjoy making it, though!

1

Stick tissue balls on with white glue to make eyes.

Blow up a balloon to 8 inches (200 mm). Tape thin card stock around its middle to make it longer. Build eyes with tissue paper.

2

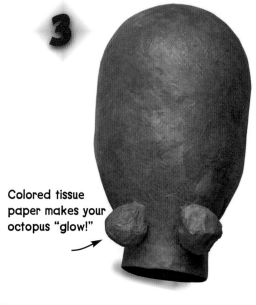

Glue several layers of paper all over the balloon and the eyes. When completely dry, pop the balloon and trim the edge.

3

Colored tissue paper makes your octopus "glow!"

Paint the body or cover it with colored tissue paper, then make a small hole in the top. Pass a piece of string through the hole.

27

4

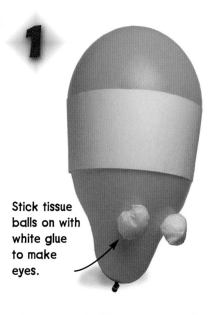

Bend your balloons before covering them!

Put slices of cork under the paper to look like suckers!

Blow up four modeling balloons. Cover them in layers of paper and allow them to dry. Cut each one in half. These are the legs. Color them with paint or tissue paper like the body.

5

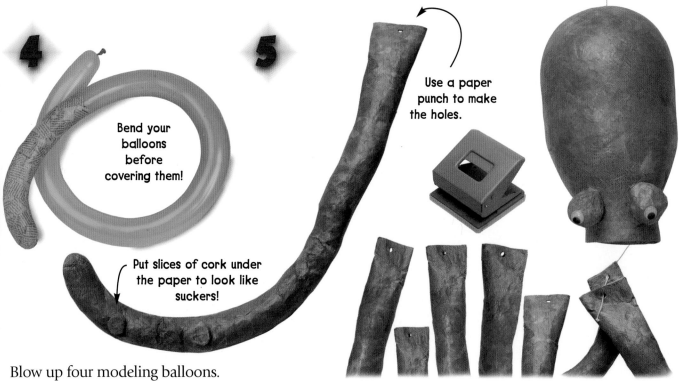

Use a paper punch to make the holes.

Flatten the tops of the legs, and punch holes through them. Pass the string through each one.

Pull the legs up into the body. Glue on some wobbly eyes. Staple a piece of elastic to the top of its head to hang it up.

Piñata

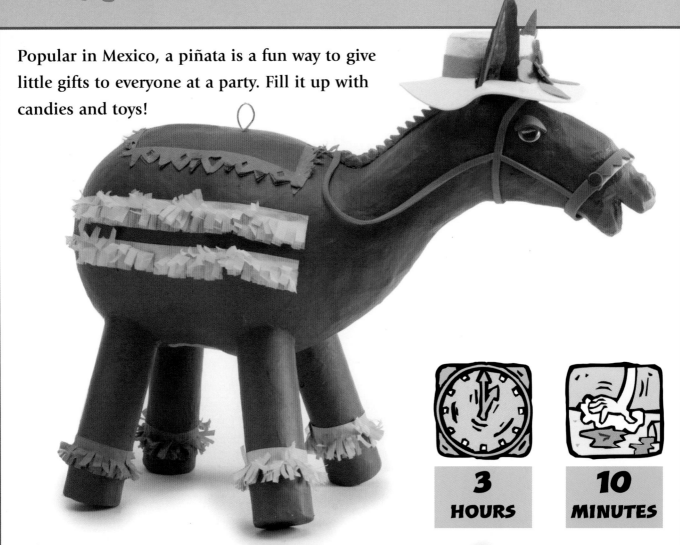

Popular in Mexico, a piñata is a fun way to give little gifts to everyone at a party. Fill it up with candies and toys!

3 HOURS

10 MINUTES

You will need:

- *One round balloon • Paper clip*
- *White glue • Long wooden stick*
- *Old newspapers • Bubble wrap*
- *Cardboard tubes • Thin card stock*
- *Colored tissue paper • Colored felt or fun foam*
- *String or elastic cord • Wobbly eyes*
- *Paints and brushes • Tape*
- *Scissors • Thumbtack • Cardboard*
- *Candies • Small toys*

What to do...

Piñata (sounds like *peen-YAH-tuh*) is the Spanish name for a decorated container. The piñata is hung up out of reach, and everyone at the party takes turns hitting it with a stick.

The winner is the one to break the piñata open, letting the contents out. It's made more fun by making the players wear a blindfold! Our piñata is shaped like a donkey.

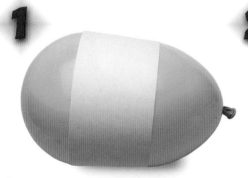

1

Blow up a round balloon and tape a piece of thin card stock around the middle to squeeze it into a longer shape. Cover it with glued paper, and set it aside to dry. This is the piñata body.

2

Cut a hole in one side of the body and pop the balloon with a thumbtack. Make a paper clip into a loop and push it up through a hole in the top of the body.

loop made from paper clip

3

Fix the loop inside with some glued paper.

Attach four cardboard tubes to the body as legs and cover them with more paper.

4

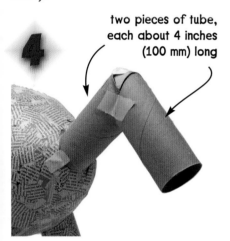

two pieces of tube, each about 4 inches (100 mm) long

Fix pieces of cardboard tube together with tape to make the head and neck.

5

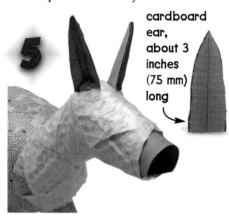

cardboard ear, about 3 inches (75 mm) long

Cut out two cardboard ears and glue them on the head. Build up the head and neck with bubble wrap, then cover with layers of glued paper.

6

Shape the muzzle with more paper.

When the paper is dry, use scissors to model the muzzle. Stick on some tissue paper to make the detailed shape.

7

Cut two 1 inch (25 mm) strips and fold in half lengthwise.

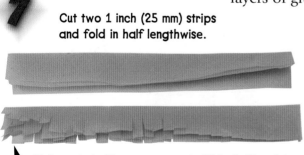

Make cuts halfway across, at .25-inch (5 mm) intervals.

Paint your piñata brown all over, and when it's dry, stick tissue paper frills on the sides and legs.

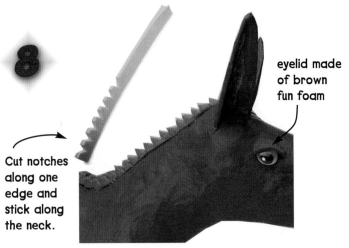

Cut notches along one edge and stick along the neck.

eyelid made of brown fun foam

Make a mane out of three strips of fun foam or felt stuck together. Stick the eyes on. Stick fun foam eyelids over the eyes.

The bridle is made of narrow strips of fun foam or felt. Glue on the noseband, then the headband and the reins.

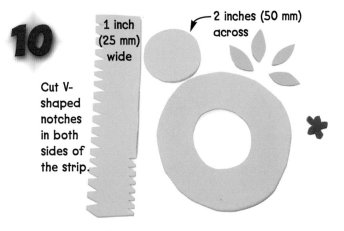

1 inch (25 mm) wide

2 inches (50 mm) across

Cut V-shaped notches in both sides of the strip.

Cut a circle in fun foam or felt about 4.5 inches (115 mm) for the brim of the hat. Cut a circle in it for the top of the crown and a strip just long enough to go around the side.

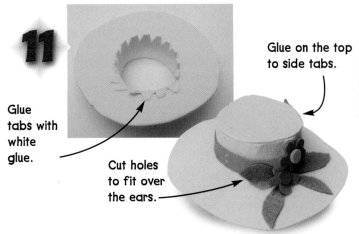

Glue tabs with white glue.

Glue on the top to side tabs.

Cut holes to fit over the ears.

Fold the tabs on the side piece and stick them on the underside of the brim. Stick the other tabs under the top piece. Arrange the parts of the flower together and stick them on with glue.

Make sure the hole is big enough for the gifts to fall out easily.

Fill the piñata with candies and toys through the hole and seal it with a single piece of tissue paper glued around the edges.

Hang up your piñata. Now you and your friends can take turns hitting the piñata with a stick!

Glossary

desert island (DEH-zert EYE-lund) An uninhabited tropical island – the kind you get shipwrecked on!

dragon (DRA-gun) A mythical beast like a giant lizard, often with claws and wings.

elastic (ih-LAS-tik) Something that can stretch and then return to its original shape.

glitter (GLIH-ter) Tiny pieces of plastic or metal with a shiny surface that catches the light.

layered (LAY-erd) Having more than one thickness of something.

maraca (MUH-rah-kuh) A hollow shell containing dried beans, peas, or stones, that make a rhythmic sound when shaken.

mobile (MOH-beel) A name for a kind of artwork made of loosely connected parts that can move around each other in movements of the air.

nylon (NY-lon) An artificial material that makes very strong, long threads.

octopus (OK-tuh-pus) A sea creature with eight arms and a balloonlike head. It has no bones.

papier-mâché (pay-per-mah-SHAY) A mixture of paper and glue that becomes very hard and strong when dry. It's a French phrase that means "chewed paper."

pattern (PA-turn) A repeated design.

piñata (peen-YAH-tuh) A kind of hollow decoration containing candies and gifts.

sequin (SEE-kwun) A small shiny disk stuck onto clothing for decoration.

shell (SHEL) A hard, hollow container.

varnish (VAHR-nish) A special liquid made to put on a surface that then dries and protects it.

Index

32

Web Sites

Due to the changing nature of Internet links, PowerKids Press has developed an online list of Web sites related to the subject of this book. This site is updated regularly. Please use this link to access the list:
www.powerkidslinks.com/myoa/papier/